Visualizing Windows 11

A Seniors' Handbook with Step-by-Step Illustrations

By

Isaac Alejo

Table of Content

Conclusion

INTRODUCTION

Windows 11 represents Microsoft's latest generation of its operating system for PCs and brings with it exciting new features and a user-friendly interface. While any change may be daunting, this guide will make the transition as smooth as possible by walking you step-by-step through everything needed to set up and use Windows 11.

This guide is designed to teach seniors the fundamentals of Windows 11, Microsoft's latest operating system. No matter your computer experience level or whether or not this is your first time with it, you will gain all of the skills needed to get up and running right away. We'll cover Windows 11 fundamentals such as using the mouse, keyboard and touchscreen. You'll learn to open apps, adjust sound settings, navigate the new Start menu and properly shut down. Mastering these basics sets a solid foundation for future accomplishments on your computer.

Learn how to create user accounts that keep your information private and safe by signing in with Microsoft or setting up separate accounts for family members. Password strength is of utmost importance when setting up user accounts for increased account security. Personalizing your Windows 11 desktop will make daily tasks simpler. Arrange apps neatly, select an eye-catching wallpaper, and use Snap Layouts to stack windows side-by-side.

Connection to the internet opens doors for shopping and entertainment as well as communicating through email. We'll explore using Microsoft Edge safely for web searches while bookmarking sites and blocking ads - you'll also learn how to shop online and order groceries or gifts! Although new technology may seem intimidating, this guide simplifies Windows 11 for beginners in clear and manageable steps.

CHAPTER 1: GETTING ACQUAINTED WITH WINDOWS 11

Tell Your Computer What to Do

How do you make Windows 11 do what you want? Well, it depends on the type of computer you have. If it's a desktop, you'll have different options compared to a handheld phone. Here are some ways you can control your computer:

- Mouse

- Touchscreen

- Keyboard

Another way to control Windows is by using a touchpad, which you can find on most laptop keyboards. It works like this: when you move your finger on the touchpad, a pointer moves on the screen accordingly.

If your computer has more than one of these control devices, you can choose to use one exclusively or switch between them based on the task you're doing. Use whatever method feels most comfortable for you, and feel free to try different options. In the following sections, you'll learn all about using these control methods in Windows 11. Once you've familiarized yourself with them, you can turn on your computer and start using these techniques.

Move the Mouse

A mouse is a small device about the size of a bar of soap that you use by moving it across a desk with your hand. When you move the mouse, you'll see an arrow on the computer screen called a mouse pointer, and it moves accordingly. There's another device called a trackball, which is like a mouse but has a ball you can rotate to move the pointer instead.

A typical mouse has two or more buttons, and some also have a scroll wheel located between the buttons.

Now, let's talk about how to use the mouse with Windows 11. Each method involves moving the mouse to position the pointer over a specific item before doing anything else:

- **Click:** To click, move the arrow-shaped mouse pointer over something you want to select and then press and release the left mouse button. It's like tapping on something.

- **Right-click:** To right-click, just press and release the right mouse button. This will show you different options or functions related to what you clicked on. Remember, clicking by itself usually means using the left mouse button.

- **Drag:** To drag something, press and hold down the left mouse button while moving the mouse pointer across the screen. This is used when you want to move an object from one place to another. When you're done, simply release the mouse button to let go of the object.

Touch the Screen

A touchscreen is a special type of screen that lets you use your fingers to interact with your computer. You can touch the screen with one finger, two fingers, or even all ten fingers. Some touchscreens also work with a special pen called a stylus. Tablets and some smartphones have touchscreens, and they are becoming more common on desktop and laptop computers too. Not sure if your computer has a touchscreen? You can gently tap the screen with your index finger while Windows 11 is running to see if it responds.

Here are some ways you can interact with a touchscreen:

- **Tap:** To select something, like a button, you just need to briefly touch it on the screen.

- **Drag:** To move an object, like an onscreen playing card, press and hold your finger on it, and then move your finger across the screen.

- **Swipe (or flick):** You can quickly move your finger across the screen to show options and commands. Swiping is like turning pages to move forward or backward. Some people call it flicking, but let's not worry too much about that.

- **Pinch and unpinch:** To make something smaller on the screen or show more content, touch the screen with a finger and thumb or two fingers and bring them closer together (pinch). To zoom in and see more detail, move your fingers away from each other (unpinch).

Use a Keyboard

A typewriter-like keyboard is a traditional way to control a computer, especially when you need to type a lot of text. There are special key combinations called shortcut keys that can help you do things quickly, but you'll need to remember them.

Here are some important keys on the keyboard:

- **Windows key:** This key is usually located on both sides of the spacebar, the big key at the bottom. It can do many things on its own or combined with other keys. We'll show you these combinations throughout the book when you might need them.

- **Tab:** Press the Tab key to highlight an item. Press it repeatedly to skip things you don't want to select.

- **Arrow keys:** These keys (left, right, up, and down) move the cursor or highlight an object in the direction they point. Sometimes, Tab and the right arrow do similar things, but it depends on the situation.

- **Enter:** Most of the time, the Enter key acts like clicking or tapping to choose a selection. But sometimes, you may need to use Tab or the arrow keys to select something before pressing Enter.

- **Ctrl, Alt, and Shift keys:** These keys work with other keys to perform commands. For example, pressing Ctrl+C copies selected text or an object. To do this, press and hold down Ctrl and then press the C key. No need to press Shift for an uppercase C. The Shift key is used to make letters uppercase.

- **Backspace:** Each press of Backspace erases the character to the left of the cursor while you're typing.

- **Delete:** Each press of the Delete key erases the character to the right of the cursor while you're typing. Some keyboards label this key as "Del."

- **Function keys:** These keys are labeled F1 through F12. You might not use them much in this book, but it's good to know where they are. On laptops, there's often a Function Lock key to turn these keys on or off.

- **Page keys:** Find the Home, End, Page Up, and Page Down keys on your keyboard for future reference. They help you move the screen, a page, or the cursor. On some keyboards, these keys also work as numbers when the Num Lock key is activated.

View the Touch Keyboard

Windows 11 has a touch keyboard that appears on the screen, which is important for devices with a touchscreen and no physical keyboard. When you see a blinking vertical bar (cursor) in a box where you can enter text, the touch keyboard will automatically pop up. If it doesn't, you might find a separate floating box near the text box, and tapping that will display the keyboard. Alternatively, you can tap the keyboard icon on the taskbar (the bar at the bottom of the screen, near the date and time) to bring up the keyboard.

To use the touch keyboard, you can simply tap or click on the letters, numbers, or symbols you want to type. There are different layouts you can use:

- **Standard Layout (QWERTY):** This layout appears automatically and is the typical keyboard layout you're familiar with. The Enter key may change depending on the context.

- **Uppercase Layout:** When you tap the Shift key on the standard layout, the uppercase layout will appear, and all letters will be capitalized.

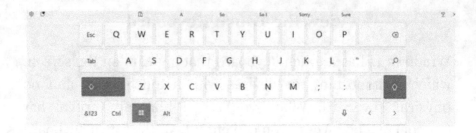

- **Numbers and Symbols Layout:** Tapping the &123 key on the standard layout will switch to this layout, allowing you to type numbers and special symbols. Tapping the &123 key again will return to the standard layout.

- **Control Keys Overlay:** If you tap the Ctrl key on the standard layout, a control keys overlay will appear on five keys (A, Z, X, C, or V). These keys are useful for tasks like copying (Ctrl+C) or moving (Ctrl+X) selected text. The overlay disappears after tapping one of the control keys.

You can customize the touch keyboard by clicking the Settings button, which looks like a gear and appears on the top left of the keyboard. From there, you can choose different keyboard layouts like Small, Split, or Traditional. You can also opt for a Handwriting option, where you can write with your finger, and Windows will convert your writing into regular text. Additionally, you can select different themes and resize options in the Personalization window.

Lastly, if you want to use emoticons while typing, you can select the emojis button and search for the emoticon you want to use. It's a fun way to add emotions to your messages.

Turn On Your Computer

1. To start your computer, you need to push the power button briefly and then release it. Every computer has a power button, and it's usually located on the front of a desktop computer tower. If you have a laptop or a different type of computer, you might find the power button on the front, sides of the screen, or near the hinges of the laptop.

2. When you turn on the computer, you might hear a beep, see some buttons light up, and the screen may briefly show a logo or message (but it will disappear quickly, so don't worry about it). After a moment, you'll see the Windows 11 Lock screen.

3. If you have any separate hardware like a monitor, speakers, or a printer, make sure to turn them on if needed.

4. Now, you'll need to enter your password and press Enter (or click the Submit button on the right side of the password box). After that, the Windows 11 desktop screen will appear, and you're all set to use your computer!

Check Out the Start Screen

1. To get started with your computer, first, make sure it's turned on, and then sign in to your user account. Once you're signed in, you'll see the Windows desktop screen.

2. To open the Start screen, you can use different methods:

   - **Mouse:** Click on the Start button, which you'll find on the taskbar at the bottom of the screen. The Start button looks like a four-pane window, and it's the leftmost icon on the taskbar.

   - **Touchscreen:** Simply tap on the Start button.

   - **Keyboard:** Press the "Windows" key, which looks like the Windows logo.

3. Now, take a look at the Start screen and notice the icons. Each icon represents an app (a program or software). Click or tap on an app icon to open that app. You can also click the Next Page button to see more apps or click the All Apps button to view an alphabetical list of all the apps installed on your computer.

4. To access more options related to your user account, click or tap on your image or name on the Start screen. This will open a pop-up menu with commands for changing account settings, locking your screen, or signing out in favor of another person who shares your computer.

5. If you want to put your computer to sleep, shut it down, or restart it, click or tap on the Power button on the Start menu. This will show a pop-up menu with these commands.

6. To close the Start screen, you can do any of the following actions:

- Click or tap the Start button again.

- Click anywhere on the desktop when the Start screen is open.

Shut Down Your Computer

1. Display the Start screen:

   - **Mouse:** Click on the Start button, which is the leftmost icon on the taskbar and looks like a four-pane window.

   - **Touchscreen:** Tap on the Start button.

   - **Keyboard:** Press the "Windows" key, which looks like the Windows logo.

2. Click or tap on the Power button located on the bottom right side of the Start menu. The Power button looks like a circle with a line through the top.

3. A pop-up box will appear with different options:

   - **Sleep:** This option reduces power consumption without closing your apps. When you wake up the computer, everything will be exactly as you left it.

   - **Shut Down:** This option exits Windows 11 and turns the computer off. It will close any apps that are currently running.

- **Restart:** This option temporarily shuts down Windows 11 and then turns it on again. It can be helpful when Windows 11 is misbehaving.

4. Choose "Shut Down" to turn off the computer.

Start Again on the Lock Screen

1. Turn on your computer. Every time you turn on your computer, the Lock screen appears. Tthe Lock screen displays the time, day, and date along with a photo.

2. Dismiss the Lock screen with one of these methods:

   - **Mouse:** Click anywhere, roll the wheel toward you, or drag the entire screen up.

   - **Touchscreen:** Drag the entire screen up.

   - **Keyboard:** Press any key.

3. If you don't use a password or Windows Hello to sign in, wait briefly for the Start screen to appear. If you use a password, enter it with a physical or touch keyboard. Then press Enter or select the arrow next to the password box to display the Windows desktop screen.

CHAPTER 2: USING THE START SCREEN, APPS, AND WIDGETS

Open Windows 11 Apps

To open the Start screen, click on the Start button on the taskbar, or you can press the "Windows" key on the keyboard. On the Start screen, you'll see a group of apps that are always there, and you can also see all the apps available on your computer by clicking the All Apps button.

1. Let's try opening the Weather app. Click on All Apps, locate the Weather app, and select it. The Weather app will show you the current temperature and weather forecast for your default location. To access more options in the app, click on the Show Options button in the upper-left corner. This will expand the app bar and display the names of the options. Click on the Show Options button again to collapse the options.

2. Now, let's switch back to the Start screen. You can do this by clicking the Start button again or pressing the "Windows" key. To go back to the Weather app, click on its title bar with the mouse or your finger (if you have a touchscreen). This will bring the Weather app back to the front, and the Start screen will disappear.

3. To open the Microsoft Edge browser, find its icon on the Start screen and click on it. Once the Edge screen appears, you can scroll down to see more content on the web page you're visiting. To scroll, you can either

drag the scroll box on the right side of the screen with the mouse, use the mouse wheel (if your mouse has one), or simply swipe up or down on the touchscreen.

4. Finally, when you're done using Edge and the Weather app, you can close them in one of these ways:

- **Mouse:** Click on the Close button (the X) in the upper-right corner of the app's window.

- **Touchscreen:** Tap on the Close button (the X) in the upper-right corner of the app's window.

- **Keyboard:** Press Alt+F4.

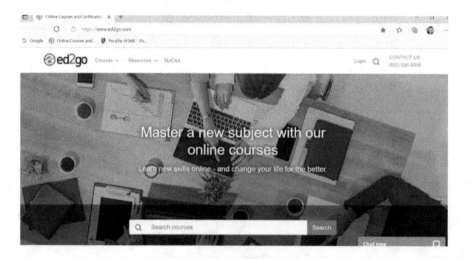

Use the App Bar

1. To start, make sure you're on the Start screen. If the Weather app is not already open, find its icon on the Start screen and click on it to open it.

2. The Weather app has something called the app bar, which has specific functions for the app you are using. To see the app bar, click on the Show Options button in the Weather app.

3. In the Weather app, you can use the app bar to access different functions. For example, you can select Maps to see a weather map of the area where you live.

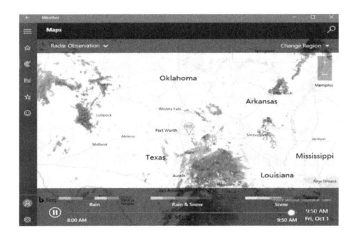

4. To see more options in the Weather app, display the app bar again and choose Historical Weather. This will show you weather trends over the past 12 months.

5. If you ever want to go back to the main screen of the Weather app, just display the app bar again and look for the Home icon. By selecting this icon, you can always return to the app's home screen, no matter where you are in the app.

Add a Location in Weather

1. Make sure you're on the Start screen. If the Weather app isn't open yet, find its icon on the Start screen and click on it to open it.

2. Once the Weather app is on the screen, look for the Show Options button and click on it. This will expand the app bar and show the names of different options.

3. Next, click on the Favorites button on the app bar. This will take you to the Favorites screen, and you'll see a different Launch Location.

4. To add a location to your favorites, click on the Add to Favorites icon. It looks like a plus sign inside a square. This will bring up the Add to Favorites screen.

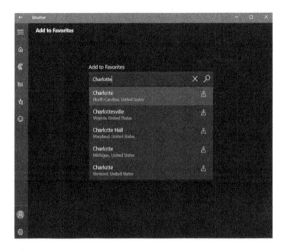

5. Type the name of the location you want to add, like a city, in the box under Add to Favorites. As you type, matching location names will appear below the box. If you see the location you want, simply click on that name to add an icon for that location to the Places screen. You don't need to click the Add button unless your location doesn't appear automatically.

6. Once you've added the location, click on the icon for that location. The Weather app will now display full information for the location you selected.

Change App Settings

1. To start, go to the Start screen and click on the Weather icon if you don't see the Weather app open already.

2. In the Weather app, look for the Settings button on the app bar. The Settings screen will appear when you select it. The Settings button is at the bottom of the app

bar. If you can't find it, click on the Show Options button, which is at the top of the app bar, to see all the buttons.

3. On the Settings screen, you can choose whether to see air temperatures in Fahrenheit or Celsius. Pick the one you prefer.

4. Next, choose a Launch Location option. If you select "Always Detect My Location," the Weather app will use your internet connection to figure out where you are currently and give you the weather report for that place. If you choose "Default Location," you can enter the name of the place where you live, and the Weather app will show you weather forecasts for that location.

Search for an App

1. Open the Start screen. At the top of the screen, you'll see a Search box. You can click on the Search box to

type a search, and when you do, the screen will automatically change to the Search screen.

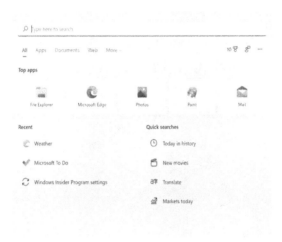

2. Alternatively, you can simply select the Search icon on the taskbar to start a search for an app or anything else you need.

3. In the Search box, type the first four letters of the word "calculator," which is "calc." As you type, the Search window will show you the results of your search.

4. To finish typing the word "calculator," add "ulator" to the search box. The Search panel will list only items with the complete word "calculator" in them, including the Calculator app.

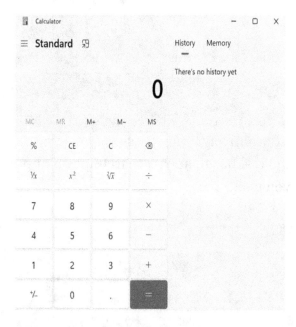

5. Now, select the Calculator app to open it on the desktop. You can use the buttons on the screen or your keyboard to perform calculations.

6. When you're done using the Calculator app, simply select the Close button to close it.

Pin and Unpin Apps on the Start Screen

To begin, open the Start screen on your computer. You'll see several apps already pinned there for easy access. However, you might not want some of these apps to be pinned, and there may be other apps you want to add.

To change the pinned apps, follow these steps:

1. Click on the All Apps button to see a list of all the apps available on your computer.

2. Look for the Calculator app in the alphabetical list.

3. To pin the Calculator app to the Start screen, you can use one of these methods:

    - **Mouse:** Right-click on the Calculator icon.

    - **Touchscreen:** Touch and hold the Calculator icon until a context menu appears, then release your finger.

4. On the context menu, choose "Pin to Start."

5. Now, select the Back button to go back to the main window of the Start screen. The Calculator app is now pinned to your Start screen and can be found in the Pinned group.

To unpin the Calculator app from the Start screen, do the following:

1. Display the context menu for the Calculator app again (right-click with the mouse or touch and hold on the touchscreen).

2. Choose "Unpin from Start" on the context menu.

Arrange Apps on the Start Screen

1. You can easily change the order of icons on the Start screen. To do this, simply drag the Calculator icon to a different location. As you move the icon, other icons

will move out of the way, just like in a game of Dodge Icon.

2. To drag an app icon, use your left mouse key to click and hold the icon, then move it to a new location among your Pinned apps. If you're using a touchscreen, press and hold the app's icon with your finger, and then drag it to the new spot.

3. Keep doing this until you have organized the app icons in a way that makes sense to you. For example, you might want to arrange the apps in a list based on how often you use them, from most frequent to least frequent, or you could organize them in alphabetical order. You can rearrange the pinned apps at any time by following these steps again.

Uninstall an App

1. Open the Start screen on your computer.

2. Look for the app you want to uninstall in the list of apps. They are listed in alphabetical order.

3. To access the app icon's context menu, you can use one of these methods:

   - **Mouse:** Right-click on the app's icon.

   - **Touchscreen:** Touch and hold the app's icon until a context menu appears, then release your finger.

4. On the context menu, you'll see the option "Uninstall." Click on "Uninstall."

5. A dialog box will appear, letting you know that the app will be removed. Click on the "Uninstall" button on the dialog box to confirm the uninstallation. The app will then be removed from your computer.

Remove and Reorganize Widgets

To start, open the Widgets panel by clicking on the Widgets icon on the taskbar.

Once you have the Widgets panel open, you can rearrange the widgets to display them in a different order. There's no right or wrong way to do it, so just organize them in a way that works best for you. To move a widget to a new spot on the panel, hover your mouse over the widget until you see a hand icon. If you're using a touchscreen, simply hold your finger on the widget. Then, drag the widget to the new location, and the other widgets will move aside to make room.

If you want to remove a widget from the panel, follow these steps:

1. Select the See Options button, which you can find in the upper right corner of the widget.

2. A menu will appear, and you should choose "Remove Widget."

Customize a Widget

1. To start, click on the Widgets icon on the taskbar. This will open the Widgets panel. In this panel, you can change the size of each widget. To do this, click on the See Options menu found in the upper right corner of the widget. You'll have three size options to choose from: Small, Medium, or Large.

2. By default, all the widgets are set to Small. To change the size of a widget, simply select the desired size from the See Options menu. You can have widgets of different sizes.

3. Additionally, you have the option to customize the data displayed on each widget. The available customization options depend on the specific widget and its functionality. For instance, if you want to add the Traffic widget to your widgets (in case it's not already

there), you can do so. After adding it, click on See Options and choose Customize Widget.

4. In the customization window, you can enter a specific location, like a city and state, or you can let the widget detect your location automatically. The second option is useful if you travel frequently as it ensures the widget always shows accurate information wherever you are. After making your desired selection, remember to click on Save to apply the changes.

CHAPTER 3: ADJUSTING WINDOWS 11 SETTINGS

Access the Settings Screen

First, click on the Search button on the taskbar.

1. Then, type "Settings" in the search bar and choose the Settings app from the search results.

2. When the Settings screen appears, you can use it to make changes to various settings on your computer.

3. To explore the options, click on each icon one by one, starting with "System." This will show you the available settings for that category. If you want to go back to the main Settings screen after exploring a category, click on the Back button, which looks like a left-pointing arrow in the upper-left corner of the screen.

4. To find printer-related settings, type "printer" in the Search box on the Settings screen. As you type, the screen will show you a list of settings related to printers. You can select any setting from the list to open the dialog box where that specific setting is located.

Personalize the Lock Screen

1. Go to the Settings screen and select "Personalization."

2. On the Personalization screen, scroll down and click on "Lock Screen" on the right side.

3. The Lock Screen Preview screen will open, and you'll see a drop-down menu called "Personalize Your Lock Screen" with three options:

   - **Windows Spotlight:** Microsoft chooses beautiful images that change frequently, providing a nice variety of nature photos.

   - **Picture:** You can choose a photo from your PC's collection, like the ones in your Pictures folder.

   - **Slideshow:** This option lets you set up a rotating collection of photos for your Lock screen, but they all need to be in the same folder on your computer.

4. If you choose the "Picture" option, you'll see recent images you can select from. If you want a specific

photo, you can click the "Browse Photos" button to find it.

5. After you select a picture, it will appear on your Lock Screen. If you ever want to change it, just repeat these steps and pick a new picture. Alternatively, you can also choose the "Slideshow" or "Windows Spotlight" options for a different look.

Choose an Account Picture

1. First, open the Settings screen. You can find how to do this earlier in this chapter if you need help.

2. Once on the Settings screen, click on "Accounts" in the left panel.

3. On the right side, you'll see a section called "Your Info" with your current account picture. If you haven't selected a picture yet, it might be just an outline.

4. To choose one of your photos as your account picture, click on the "Browse Files" button. This will show the contents of your Pictures folder in a window called the "Open dialog box."

5. You can use the File Explorer navigation pane to access any folder on your computer or select a subfolder to open.

6. When you find the picture you want, click on it, and then click the "Choose Picture" button. If you change

your mind, you can click "Cancel" to go back without making any changes.

7. Alternatively, if your computer has a built-in or attached camera (a webcam), you can select the "Open Camera" button. This will open the Camera app with a preview of what your camera sees.

8. After you've selected a picture or taken a new one with your camera, go back to the Start screen to see your new account picture. You can do this by clicking on the Start button or pressing the Windows key on your keyboard.

Check for Important Updates

1. Open the Settings screen, and to find out how to do this, you can check the instructions earlier in this chapter.

2. Once on the Settings screen, click on "Windows Update" on the left side. This will take you to the Windows Update screen.

3. On the Windows Update screen, you'll see information about when Windows 11 last checked for updates and if any updates were found.

4. To check for updates manually, click on the "Check for Updates" button. This will let you know if there are any

available updates for your computer, and you can update Windows 11 if needed.

5. Sometimes, certain updates require your computer to shut down and restart. If this is the case, you'll see a "Restart Now" button on the Windows Update screen. You can click on it to install the updates immediately, or you can simply wait until the next time you shut down and restart your computer on your own, and the updates will be installed then.

6. Windows 11 may automatically download and install some updates without requiring any action from you. If you see a message about automatic updates, you don't need to do anything. Windows will manage those updates on its own.

Make Windows 11 Easier to Use

To make your computer, mouse, and monitor easier to use, you can adjust settings in the Accessibility section of the Settings screen. Here's how:

- Open the Settings screen and select "Accessibility."

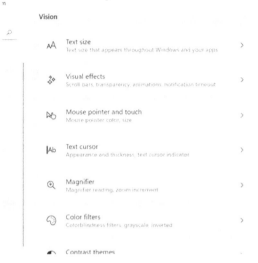

- In the Accessibility screen, you'll find various settings organized into three categories: Vision, Hearing, and Interaction.

For Vision:

- To change the text size and make it easier to read, choose "Text Size" settings under Vision.

- To customize the appearance of the mouse pointer, select "Mouse Pointer and Touch" settings.

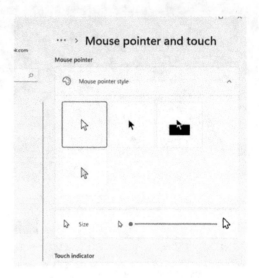

- If you want to change the color and thickness of the text cursor, choose "Text Cursor" settings.

- For better visibility, use the "Magnifier" settings to enlarge parts of your screen.

- If you are color blind, you can choose a Color Filter that suits your type of color blindness.

- To adjust the screen's contrast for easier text viewing, use the "Contrast Themes" settings.

- To have the content on your screen read aloud, turn on "Narrator" settings and customize the voice.

For Hearing:

- To increase the volume and control sound options, choose "Audio Settings" under Hearing.

- If you need subtitles in audio and video presentations, you can customize "Captions" settings, including font, background, and window appearance.

For Interaction:

- To dictate text instead of typing and control your computer with voice commands, select "Speech" settings.

- You can use an onscreen keyboard if you don't have a physical one by choosing "Keyboard" settings.

- If needed, you can control the mouse using the numeric keypad with "Mouse" settings.

- For advanced interaction, you can use "Eye Control" with an eye-tracking device. You can find more information about setting up and using this feature by selecting the provided link on the screen.

Customize the Start Menu

1. Open the Settings screen, and if you need help with this, you can check the instructions earlier in this chapter.

2. Once on the Settings screen, select "Personalization."

3. In the Personalization section, click on "Start." This will open the Personalization > Start screen.

4. On the Start screen, you have a few options to customize it according to your preferences. You can turn the following items on or off:

    - **Show Recently Added Apps:** This will display the names of recently installed apps on the Start menu.

- **Show Most Used Apps:** This will show the names of the programs you use most frequently under the "Recommended" section on the Start menu.

- **Show Recently Opened Items in Jump Lists on Start or the Taskbar and in File Explorer:** This allows you to quickly open folders, files, and windows from the Start menu, taskbar, or File Explorer screen. When you hover the pointer over an app or program on the Start menu, an arrow appears, and you can select it to see a menu of items you can open. On the taskbar, thumbnail windows appear when you hover over an icon, letting you choose which window to open. In File Explorer, the items are listed in the Quick Access section of the navigation pane.

- **Folders:** This option lets you add specific folders to the Start menu. After you place them there, they will appear next to the Power button. For example, you can add your Documents or Pictures folder for quick and easy access.

Handle Notifications

1. Open the Settings screen, and if you need help with this.

2. Once on the Settings screen, select "System."

3. In the System section, click on "Notifications."

4. Under "Notifications," you'll see a list of apps and other senders that can show notifications. You can turn options on or off to decide if you want these notifications to appear on your screen.

5. To make your choices, simply switch the options on or off as you prefer.

6. Once you've set your notification preferences, click on the Close button (the X) to close the Settings window.

CHAPTER 4: WORKING WITH USER ACCOUNTS

Connect to the Internet

To check if your computer is connected to the internet, look for the Network icon on the bottom-right corner of the screen, next to the time and date.

1. Click on the Network icon, and a panel will appear on the right side of the screen showing the network you are connected to.

2. To see available Wi-Fi networks, click on the Wi-Fi button in the network panel.

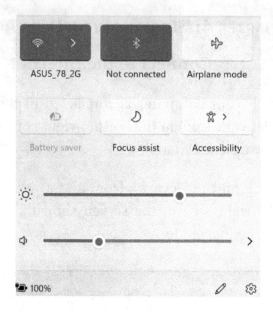

3. Choose the Wi-Fi network you want to connect to from the list displayed.

4. Once you select a network, an option to "Connect Automatically" may appear. If you trust the network and want to use it again in the future, check the box. If not, leave it unchecked. Then, click the "Connect" button to proceed.

5. If the network is secure, you may be prompted to enter a network security key (a series of characters). This key ensures that only authorized users can access the network. If you have the key, enter it, and click "Next." If you don't know the key or are using a public network, click "Cancel."

6. After establishing a Wi-Fi connection, the word "Connected" will appear next to the network name in the Networks panel. You'll also see the connection strength near the time and date in the lower-right corner of the screen.

Keep in mind that if you're connecting to a public network, it's generally a good idea to select "No" when asked about turning on sharing between PCs and devices to protect your computer from unauthorized access. At home or in a trusted environment, you can choose "Yes" to share documents and devices between your computers on the network.

Disconnect (or Switch to Airplane Mode)

When you turn off your computer or move it away from the internet connection, it automatically disconnects from the internet. But sometimes, you might want to disconnect it yourself. Here's how:

1. To disconnect your computer from the internet, click on the network icon on the taskbar. This will show the network panel.

2. If you want to turn off Wi-Fi, simply click on the Wi-Fi button. When you do this, the button will change from blue to white, indicating that Wi-Fi is now off, and your computer is disconnected from the internet. To reconnect, click the Wi-Fi button again, and it will turn blue, signifying that Wi-Fi is on, and your computer can connect to the internet again. Make sure to reconnect before you proceed to Step 3.

3. When you are on an airplane, the airline asks you to turn off electronic devices to avoid interfering with the airplane's communication systems. Instead of turning off your computer completely, you can switch to

"Airplane mode." To do this, open the network panel and click on the Airplane Mode button, which is located at the top right of the network panel.

4. In Airplane mode, you'll see an airplane icon next to the time and date in the lower-right corner of the screen. This mode ensures that your computer doesn't send any wireless signals, making it safe to use during the flight.

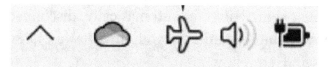

5. To switch back to regular mode and reconnect to the internet, click on the airplane icon to show the network panel again. Then, click the Airplane Mode button to turn it off.

Create a New Microsoft Account

1. To create a Microsoft Account, start by going to the Start screen and selecting your picture on the left side of the screen. Then, choose "Change Account Settings" from the pop-up menu that appears.

2. If you see the words "Local Account" under your name, it means you're signed in with a local account. To switch to a Microsoft Account, select the "Sign In with a Microsoft Account Instead" link.

3. On the Sign In screen, you can either use an email address or a phone number to create the account. If you choose the email option, type in the email address you want to use and follow the prompts. If you prefer to use your phone number, select "Use a Phone Number Instead" and enter your phone number.

4. Next, create a password for your Microsoft Account. Remember to use at least eight characters with a combination of uppercase letters, lowercase letters, numbers, or symbols.

5. Enter your first and last name, then provide your birth date and country or region.

6. Review your entries, and if everything is correct, select "Next."

7. You'll receive a verification code from Microsoft via email or text message. Enter that code on the Verify screen.

8. Finally, on the "Sign In to This Device Using Your Microsoft Account" screen, enter the username and password of your local account (if you have one). Then click "Next."

9. Congratulations! You've successfully created a Microsoft Account..

Create a Local Account

1. Before you start, make sure to save any work you have open.

2. Click on the Start button and then click on your picture on the Start menu.

3. In the pop-up menu that appears, choose "Sign in with a local account instead."

4. Click on the "Sign In with a Local Account Instead" link.

5. You'll see the "Switch to a Local Account" screen. Click on the "Skip This Step" button and then click "Next" on the following screen.

6. On the "Making Sure It's You" screen, enter the password of your Microsoft Account, and then click "OK."

7. Next, you'll be asked to enter a user name, a password (twice), and a hint to help you remember the password. Once you've filled those in, click "Next."

8. Click on the "Sign Out and Finish" button. This will close your Microsoft Account, and Windows will restart.

9. After the restart, you'll see the Windows 11 screen. Enter the password you created in Step 3.

Switch from a Local to an Existing Microsoft Account

1. Go to the Start screen, and in the bottom-left corner, you'll see your name. Click on it.

2. A pop-up menu will appear. Choose "Change Account Settings."

3. The Accounts screen will open, and you'll see your account information with "Local Account" under your name.

4. Click on the "Sign In with a Microsoft Account Instead" link.

5. Next, type in the email address or phone number associated with your Microsoft Account, and click on the "Next" button. Make sure you are connected to the internet to sign in with a Microsoft account.

6. Enter the password for your Microsoft Account, and click on the "Sign In" button.

7. You'll be asked to enter the password of your current local account in the "Current Windows Password" text box. After entering it, click on the "Next" button.

8. The Accounts screen will open again, showing the user name and email address of your Microsoft Account.

Create a Local Account for Someone in Your Household

1. Go to the Start screen and click on your name.

2. From the menu that appears, choose "Change Account Settings." This will open the Settings app to the Accounts screen.

3. On the left side, select "Accounts," and on the right side, choose "Family & Other Users."

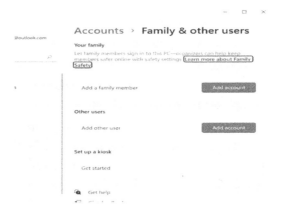

4. Next, click on "Add account" next to "Add Other User." This will take you to the "How Will This Person Sign In" screen.

5. At the bottom of this screen, click on the link called "I Don't Have This Person's Sign-In Information."

6. On the next screen, select "Add a User without a Microsoft Account."

7. Now, you'll be on the "Create a User for This PC" screen. Enter a user name in the first box, something easy to remember and type, like the person's first name, last name, or nickname.

8. In the Password box, you can create a password for the account (or skip to Step 9 if you don't want to set a password). Each character you type will be shown as a dot for security.

9. Reenter the password in the "Reenter Password" box to confirm it.

10. In the three drop-down menus, choose a security question and provide the answer. This will be used to recover your password if you forget it.

11. Once you've filled in all the required information, click the "Next" button. The new user name will now appear under "Other Users" in the Accounts screen.

12. Return to the Start screen and click on your user name. You'll notice the new user name appears on the drop-down menu. You can switch between accounts by selecting a user name from the drop-down menu. To sign out of an account, choose "Sign Out."

13. To switch to the new user account, select the user name from the drop-down menu.

14. A screen will appear with the new user name. If you used a password for the new account, type it in the box and click the onscreen right arrow or press Enter. If there's no password, simply click the "Sign In" button.

Create a Password for a Local Account

1. If you are not already signed in to the local account, sign in first.

2. Go to the Start screen and click on your name.

3. From the drop-down menu that appears, choose "Change Account Settings." This will open the Settings app to the Accounts screen.

4. Select "Sign-in Options."

5. Then, click on "Password."

6. If you don't have a password but want to set one, click the "Add" button under "Password."

7. On the "Create a Password" screen, type a password of your choice in the "New Password" box.

8. Reenter the same password in the "Reenter Password" box to confirm it.

9. Provide a hint that will help you remember the password, but make sure it's something only you can understand. Don't include the actual password in the hint.

10. Once everything is filled in, click "Finish." If there are any error messages, correct the entries and click "Next" again.

Change or Remove a Local Account Password

1. First, sign in to the local account with the current password you want to change or remove.

2. Go to the Start screen and click on your name.

3. From the drop-down menu that appears, choose "Change Account Settings." This will open the Settings app to the Accounts screen.

4. On the left side of the Accounts screen, select "Sign-in Options."

5. In the middle of the screen, click on "Password."

6. Select the "Change" button.

7. On the "Change Your Password" screen, enter your current password and then click "Next."

8. On the next screen, enter the new password you want. If you don't want to have a password, simply click "Next" and skip to Step 9.

9. Reenter the new password in the "Reenter Password" box to confirm it.

10. Add a hint that will help you remember your password, but make sure it's something only you can understand. Then click "Next." If there are any error messages, correct the entries and click "Next" again.

11. The final screen will indicate that you must use your new password the next time you sign in. (This message will appear even if you left the password blank, in which case you won't need any password.) Click "Finish."

Delete a Local Account

1. Go to the Start screen and click on your name.

2. Choose "Change Account Settings." This will take you to the Your Info page in the Settings screen.

3. Make sure it says "administrator" under your name. You need to be the computer's administrator to delete a local account.

4. On the Accounts screen, select "Family & Other Users."

5. Choose the account you want to delete from the list, and then click the "Remove" button.

6. In the Delete Account and Data window, click the "Delete Account and Data" button.

Chapter 5: Getting Comfortable with the Desktop

Check Out the Desktop

To go to the desktop on your computer, you can do any of the following:

- Press the Windows key + D.

- Right-click on the Windows button and choose "Desktop" from the menu that appears.

1. Once you are on the desktop, you will see a picture in the background. Look for icons on the desktop - these are small pictures representing either programs (like games or software) or documents (like letters or photos). You can click on an icon to open a program or document. You'll also find an icon for the Recycle Bin, where deleted files go. This might be the only icon on your desktop, or there could be more.

2. At the bottom of the screen, you'll see the taskbar. It has the following features from left to right:

   - **Start button:** Clicking on this button opens the Start screen. Click it again to close the Start screen.

   - **Search button:** You can click on this button to open the Search screen and search for Windows settings, applications, files on your computer, and information on the Internet.

- **Virtual Desktop:** This button allows you to create additional virtual desktops for better organization (learn more in "Open a Second Desktop" later in this chapter).

- **Icons:** Some icons appear automatically on the taskbar, such as File Explorer and Edge. Clicking on these icons opens the respective programs. When you open an application, its icon will also appear on the taskbar.

- **System tray:** The system tray displays icons for programs that run automatically when your computer starts. On the right side of the system tray, you'll see the date and time. The Notification icon is also located there.

3. You can use the taskbar to switch among different programs by clicking on the icon for the program you want to use.

4. If you right-click or tap and hold on an icon, a small box will appear with options related to that icon. You can dismiss this box by clicking anywhere else on the desktop. Try right-clicking on different areas of the screen to see how the options in the context menu change.

Apps and Features
Mobility Center
Power Options
Event Viewer
Device Manager
Network Connections
Disk Management
Computer Management
Windows Terminal
Windows Terminal (Admin)
Task Manager
Settings
File Explorer
Search
Run
Shut down or sign out   >
Desktop

Change the Date or Time

1. Click on the date and time displayed on the taskbar. A calendar will pop up.

2. If the date or time is incorrect for your location, you can fix it by searching for "Date and Time settings." To do this, click on the Search button on the taskbar and

type "Date and Time settings" in the search box. Then, select the option that appears in the search results. Alternatively, you can right-click on the date and time in the system tray and choose "Adjust Date & Time."

3. The Settings screen will open, and you'll see the Date & Time window. By default, Windows 11 automatically sets the correct time and date from the Internet. However, if it's not accurate, you can turn off the "Set Time Automatically" option and click on the "Change" button. This will take you to the "Change Date and Time" screen.

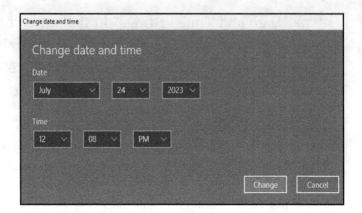

4. On the "Change Date and Time" screen, select the correct date and time. You can change the time using the little triangles that point up (to set it later) or down (to set it earlier), or you can enter the specific hours and minutes manually. Once you've made the adjustments, click "Change" to apply the changes, or click "Cancel" to keep the current settings.

5. Back in the Date and Time window, make sure to select your Time Zone from the drop-down list if it's not already correct. If you live in an area where daylight saving time is observed, you'll also find a toggle button for "Adjust for Daylight Saving Time." Keep this button turned on if you want your computer to automatically adjust for daylight saving time changes.

Explore the Parts of a Window

1. To open File Explorer, click on the icon that looks like a folder on the taskbar.

File Explorer will open, and you'll see a window with various elements:

- **Title bar:** The top line of the window shows the name of the file or folder that is currently open.

- **Toolbar:** The toolbar provides quick access to common tools, such as Cut, Copy, Paste, Sort, View, and others.

- **Minimize:** The Minimize button, located in the upper-right corner, makes the window smaller and hides its contents. The program is still running, and you'll see its icon on the taskbar. Use this button when you want to temporarily ignore a window but keep it open. To restore the window, click its icon on the taskbar.

- **Maximize/Restore:** The Maximize button (a single square in the upper-right corner) expands the window to fill the screen, giving you a better view of its contents. The Restore button (two squares in the upper-right corner) appears after you select Maximize and returns the window to its previous size.

- **Close:** The Close button (an X in the upper-right corner) is used to close the window when you're done with it.

- **Window Contents**: The main part of the window displays the program or document you're using. In File Explorer, the left side shows locations (like drives and folders), and the right side shows the objects in that location.

- **Status bar:** The bottom edge of the window may show a status bar in some programs, providing information about the window or its contents. In File Explorer, it shows how many files are in the currently open folder and how many files are selected.

2. Remember to check the edges of windows as important information and functions might be located there.

3. To close File Explorer, simply click the Close button (the X) in the upper-right corner of the window.

Resize a Window

1. To change the size of a window, first, open File Explorer by clicking on the folder icon in the taskbar.

2. If the window is taking up the whole screen (maximized), click the Restore button to make it smaller.

3. To resize the window, you can use one of these methods:

- **Mouse:** Move your mouse pointer to the right edge of the window until it turns into a double-headed arrow (resize pointer). Click and hold the mouse button while dragging the edge of the window to make it bigger or smaller.

- **Touchscreen:** If you have a touchscreen device, simply drag the right edge of the window with your finger to resize it.

4. If you want to change both the width and height of the window together, drag any of the corners of the window. But be careful not to accidentally click the Close button in the top-right corner while resizing.

5. You can also resize the window's width or height separately by dragging any of the four sides.

6. Feel free to leave the window open as you move on to the next task.

Arrange Some Windows

1. To open the Recycle Bin, go to the desktop and double-click or double-tap its icon. The Recycle Bin is like a storage area for deleted files and folders. It will open in a separate window called File Explorer.

2. If File Explorer is not already open, you can open it by clicking on the folder icon on the taskbar. Now you will see two windows on the desktop: one is titled "This PC" and the other is titled "Recycle Bin."

3. You can move the Recycle Bin window a little by dragging its title bar (the top bar of the window) without touching the buttons on the left and right ends.

4. Similarly, you can move the "This PC" window by dragging its title bar. When you move it, it will appear in front of the Recycle Bin window. Try moving both windows so that you can see a little bit of each.

5. You can practice moving both windows around. Arranging windows like this allows you to see and work with more than one thing at a time on your computer. You can also use the techniques you learned in the previous section about resizing windows to see as much as possible of both windows at the same time.

6. Keep both windows open for the next task you want to do.

Use Snap Layouts

1. Open the File Explorer window and the Recycle Bin by double-clicking their icons on the desktop. You can also open the Edge browser and the Windows Store by clicking their icons on the taskbar.

2. Now you have four different windows open on your desktop. That might seem like a lot to handle, and switching between them could be confusing and time-consuming. But don't worry! Windows 11 has a helpful feature called Snap Layouts that makes it easy to work with several windows at once.

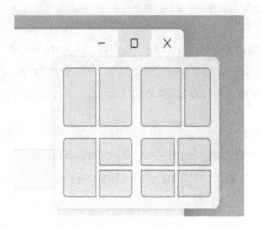

3. To use Snap Layouts, point your mouse to the Maximize button on one of the windows (it doesn't matter which one), and a pop-up menu will appear.

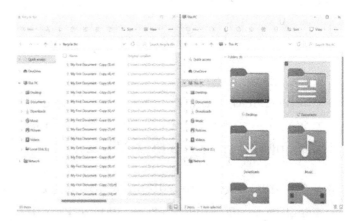

4. In the pop-up menu, you'll see different snap layout groups, each representing a specific area on the desktop where you can "snap" the selected window. For example, you can choose the left block in the first snap group and then the right block in the same group for a

second window. This will snap both windows in place side by side so you can work with them together.

5. If you have four open windows, you can choose the four-window snap layout and snap each open window to the desired location. This will arrange all four windows in a neat four-grid layout.

6. In the snap view, you can work with each window without minimizing the others. If you want to move a window out of the snap view, just drag its title bar or select the Maximize button. Then you can move the window around, resize it, or close it as you normally would. Snap Layouts make it easier to multitask and be more productive with multiple windows on your desktop.

Open a Second Desktop

1. If you don't have File Explorer and Recycle Bin open on your desktop, open them now.

2. Next, look for the Virtual Desktop button on the taskbar and select it. When you do, a small version of an open desktop will appear, and you'll see an option to create a new desktop.

3. Choose "New Desktop." Now, you'll have a brand-new, empty desktop called "Desktop 2." Congratulations, you're now on Desktop 2! You can create multiple desktops like this to keep your work organized and avoid having too many applications cluttering up one desktop. For instance, you can use one desktop for work-related apps and another for leisure activities, making it easier to find what you need.

4. While you're on Desktop 2, open the Photos app. With just one application on the desktop, it's simpler to work with.

5. To switch back to Desktop 1 (the original and only open desktop), move your mouse cursor or use your finger on the touchscreen to hover over the Desktop 2 tile. You'll see a "Close" button appear; click or tap on it. Now, the Photos app that you opened on Desktop 2 will appear back on Desktop 1. When you close a desktop, all its open applications will move to the desktop that is still open. This way, you can easily manage and switch between different tasks on different desktops.

Choose a Desktop Background

1. Click on the Search icon on the taskbar, and type "Settings" in the search bar. Choose the "Settings" app from the search results.

2. In the Settings app, select "Personalization." Then, in the Personalization window, click on "Background." This is where you can choose a background image for your Windows desktop.

3. In the Personalization window, click on "Picture" in the Background menu.

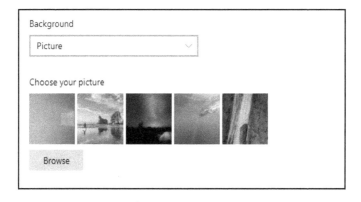

4. Select any photo you like from the options shown to set it as your desktop background. The background will change immediately. To see the entire desktop,

minimize the Settings window. If you want to go back to the Settings window, click on its icon on the taskbar or repeat the previous steps.

Pin Icons to the Taskbar

1. On the Start screen, find the Calculator icon by clicking on the All Apps button.

2. To open a menu with more options for the Calculator icon, you can do one of these things:

   - **Mouse:** Right-click the Calculator icon.

   - **Touchscreen:** Swipe the Calculator icon slightly down or up.

3. Select "More" from the menu that appears. This will show a submenu with additional options.

4. Choose "Pin to Taskbar" from the submenu. This action will add the Calculator icon to the taskbar on your desktop, making it easier to access. You will see the Calculator icon on the taskbar.

5. To remove the Calculator icon from the taskbar, repeat Steps 1 and 3, and then select "Unpin from Taskbar."

6. Now, switch to the desktop, and you will notice that the Calculator icon is no longer on the taskbar.

Stop Apps with the Task Manager

1. Click on the Search icon on the taskbar and type "Task Manager" in the search box. Then, select "Task Manager" from the search results.

2. In the Task Manager, you'll see a list of all the apps currently running on your computer, including both regular desktop apps and Windows 11 apps. If you want to stop any of these apps, you can select the app, and then you'll see the "End Task" button become available. You don't have to end any tasks right now, but you have the option to do so without any negative effects.

3. When you're done with the Task Manager, simply close it by clicking the "X" button or pressing the close button.

Browse the Web with Edge

To open Edge, click on its icon on the taskbar. When Edge opens, you'll see the start page with websites and news stories that Microsoft thinks you might be interested in, based on your browsing history. If you haven't used Edge much or at all, the suggestions on this page may not be very exciting.

1. Look at the top of the Edge screen, and you'll see the address bar. Type "www.amazon.com" in the address bar. As you type, you'll see search suggestions appear in a drop-down menu. You can either select "www.google.com" from the suggestions or press Enter. This will take you to the Dummies Press web page.

2. On the Amazon web page, you'll see store with different product categories. When you move your mouse over a link, the pointer will change to a hand, indicating it's a clickable link.

3. To go back to the previous page, click the Back button (it looks like an arrow) in the upper-left corner of the screen or press Alt+left arrow. If you want to move forward to the page you visited before, click the Forward button (it's next to the Back button) or press Alt+right arrow. Edge remembers the pages you visit, so you can easily go back and forth.

4. If you want to save the amazon.com page as a favorite, click the "Add This Page to Favorites" button on the right side of the address bar or press Ctrl+D. A panel will appear where you can click the "Add" button to add amazon.com to your Favorites list. Later, you can easily revisit your favorite websites from the Favorites list.

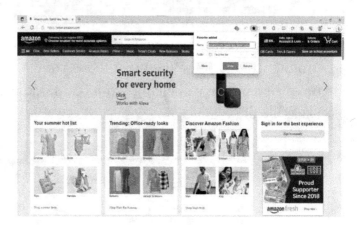

5. Leave Edge open if you want to continue with the next topic in this chapter.

Open Multiple Pages in Separate Tabs

1. If Edge is not already open, open it now.

2. Go to the Google website by typing "www.google.com" in the address bar and pressing Enter.

3. To open a new tab, click the New Tab button (it looks like a plus sign) to the right of the tabs you already have open. A new web page will appear in the middle, and a new tab called "New Tab" will appear at the top of the screen.

4. On the new tab, type "www.amazon.com" in the address bar and press Enter. Now you have two websites open in Edge. The first tab shows Google.com, and the second tab shows amazon.com. You can see the names of the web pages on the tabs.

5. If you want to go back to the Google website, click on the first tab, which has the name "Google" on it.

6. Having multiple tabs open allows you to keep one page open while you visit another. It's useful for comparing information or following different thoughts.

7. To close a tab, click the Close button (it looks like an X) on the tab you want to close. If you want to reduce clutter and simplify switching between open tabs, you can close tabs when you're done with them.

Search for Anything

1. To search for something in Edge, go to the address bar and type "travel." You might see a list of suggested search terms, but you can ignore them for now. Next, click on "Bing Search" to open the Bing website.

2. On the Bing search results page, you'll see a list of links related to your search. Scroll down to see more results and click on any link that interests you. If you reach the bottom of the page, click the "Next" button to see more search results.

3. To go back to the previous screen, click on the Back button (it looks like an arrow pointing left) or press Alt+left arrow on your keyboard.

4. If you want to search for something more specific, click on the address bar again and type "travel new mexico" (no need to use capital letters). As you type, you may see suggestions for your search, and you can click on one if it matches what you're looking for. Otherwise, press Enter to start the search.

5. On the Bing page, you'll notice tabs below the search box. The first tab is "All," which shows the default search results. You can click on other tabs like "Images," "Videos," "Maps," "News," and "Shopping" to see specific search results related to those categories.

6. Feel free to keep Edge open if you want to continue learning about the next topic.

Bookmark and Revisit Your Favorite Websites

1. To add your favorite website to Edge, first, open the Edge browser. Then, go to your favorite website on the Internet. If you don't have a favorite, you can go to www.amazon.com. When you find a website that you want to visit again easily, you can add it to your Favorites list.

2. To do this, look for the "Add This Page to Favorites" button on the right side of the address bar. It looks like a star. Click on it, and a panel will appear where you can describe the website and store its name in the Favorites list.

3. Before adding the website, you can do a couple of things:

   - Enter a shorter and more descriptive name for the website in the "Name" text box.

- Choose a folder name from the "Save In" menu to organize your favorite website in a specific folder.

4. To see if the website is added to your Favorites list, click on the "Favorites" button or press Ctrl+I. The Favorites panel will open, and you can look for your website in the list.

5. To quickly go back to the website you visited previously, click on the "Back" button in the upper-left corner of the screen. Then, click on the "Favorites" button again, and select the website you bookmarked in Step 3. The website will open on the screen.

6. You can also make the Favorites bar appear below the address bar. This way, you can easily click on a favorite

website without opening the Favorites panel. To show the Favorites bar, open the Favorites panel, click on the "See More" button, and choose "Show Favorites Bar." Any website you really like can go on the Favorites bar.

7. To manage your favorite websites, click anywhere on the screen except in the Favorites panel to close it. Then click on the "Favorites" button to open the Favorites panel. From here, you can:

   - Reorder the websites and folders by dragging them up or down in the list.

   - Remove a website or folder by right-clicking on it and choosing "Delete."

   - Create a new folder by selecting "Add Folder" on the Favorites panel toolbar and giving it a name.

   - Rename a website or folder by right-clicking on it and choosing "Rename," then enter a new name.

8. If you're ready to continue, feel free to keep Edge open as we move on to the next topic.

Explore Edge Features

1. You can customize the start screen on Edge by pinning your favorite web pages to it. First, go to your absolute favorite web page, and then select the "Settings and More" button in the upper-right corner of the screen.

From the drop-down menu, choose "More Tools," and then select "Pin to Start" from the submenu. You'll get a confirmation dialog box asking if you want to pin the web page to the Start menu, so click "Pin" to confirm.

2. After pinning the web page, you can go to the Start screen and select its tile. This will open Edge and take you directly to your favorite website. It's a convenient way to access your preferred pages quickly.

3. If you want to see the websites you visited in the past, you can select the "Settings and More" button, and then choose "History." The History panel will open, showing websites you visited in the past hour, day, or week. You can scroll down to see older websites and click on any website to open it in Edge.

4. If you prefer to browse the web privately without leaving a history, you can use the "InPrivate" browsing feature. To do this, click on the "Settings and More" button, and choose "New InPrivate Window." This will

open a separate window where your browsing activities won't be recorded in the History panel.

5. Additionally, Edge has a feature called Collections that lets you save interesting things you find on the web for later. To use Collections, click on the "Collections" button on the Edge toolbar, and then follow the instructions to create and organize collections of web pages, images, and notes.

6. You can create as many collections as you want, and it's a useful way to keep track of information you want to revisit later.

7. Finally, you can close Edge or keep reading to learn how to turn off ads on web pages if you're interested.

Block Ads on Web Pages

1. When you spend time on the web, you might notice annoying ads that get in the way of your browsing. But don't worry, there's a way to get rid of them! You can do this by installing an app called Adblock Plus from the

Microsoft Store. It's free and easy to install, taking only about half a minute.

2. To get started, close the Edge browser and go to the Microsoft Store. Search for "Adblock Plus" and click on the install button to add it to your computer.

3. Once Adblock Plus is installed, open Edge again. You'll see a confirmation message that the app is installed. You can close this message and go to any web page you want to visit.

4. When you open a web page, you might notice a large ad at the top. However, after installing Adblock Plus, this ad will be gone. You'll also see the Adblock Plus button (with the letters ABP) on the toolbar. This button shows the number of ads that have been blocked on the page you're currently visiting.

5. If you ever come across a web page that doesn't work properly because of ad blocking, you can turn off Adblock Plus temporarily. Just click the ABP button, slide the slider to the left, and select the Refresh button to reload the page without ad blocking.

6. To close the Adblock Plus menu, simply click or tap anywhere on the web page. That's it! Now you can enjoy a more pleasant and ad-free browsing experience.

CHAPTER 7: EMAILING FAMILY AND FRIENDS

Use the Mail App

To access your email on Windows 11, look for the Mail icon on the taskbar. If you can't find it there, click on the Search icon, type "mail" in the search box, and select the Mail app from the results. The Mail app will open.

If you are signed in to your Microsoft Account, the Mail app will already know your email address, which will be displayed on the Mail screen. You are now ready to use your email. If you are not signed in with a Microsoft Account, you'll need to enter your email address and password on the Sign In screen to access your email.

Once you open the Mail app, you'll land in the Inbox folder. If you haven't used your Microsoft Account for email yet, you might not have any messages in your Inbox. However, you may see a message or two from Microsoft.

To see all your email folders, select the Expand/Collapse button on the Inbox screen. This will expand the Folders panel, where you can view the names of all your folders. The Mail app organizes your emails into different folders.

Here are some important folders you might see in the Folders panel:

1. **Outbox:** Contains email you have sent or are in the process of sending.

2. **Inbox:** Displays email you have received and haven't moved to other folders, including both read and unread emails.

3. **Archive:** Used to store emails you want to keep for reference.

4. **Drafts:** Where you can save email drafts until you are ready to send them.

5. **Sent:** Stores copies of the emails you have sent.

6. **Deleted:** Contains messages you have deleted from your Inbox. You can retrieve messages from this folder if you change your mind.

7. **Conversation History:** Keeps track of entire email conversations with people, making it easier to follow conversations over time.

8. **Junk:** Messages suspected of being spam or unwanted email are moved here instead of your Inbox.

You may also see other folders in the Folders panel if you have linked the Mail app to other email accounts with additional folders.

To write an email, proceed to the next section.

Write an Email Message

1. To write a new email in the Mail app, click on the New Mail button, which looks like a plus sign, in the top-left corner of the screen. It doesn't matter which folder you're in when you click this button. The Compose screen will appear.

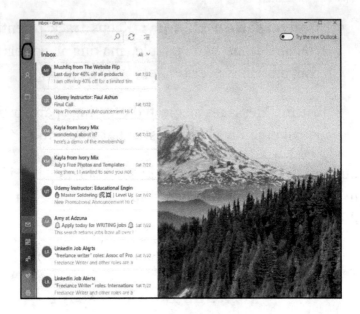

2. Type the recipient's email address in the "To" box. If you've previously emailed this person, the Mail app may recognize their address and show it as a suggestion for you to select.

3. Next, enter a short description of your email's content or purpose in the "Subject" box.

4. Click below the Subject line to start typing your actual message. Avoid writing in all capital letters as it may come across as shouting.

5. When you're done composing your email, click the "Send" button located in the top-right corner of the

Compose window to send your message. If you change your mind and don't want to send the email, you can click the "Discard" button.

6. After sending the email, you'll return to the folder you were in before starting to compose the email. You can repeat these steps to write and send more emails as needed.

Format Email

1. First, select the text you want to format. You can do this in different ways:

- If you're using a mouse, click and drag the mouse pointer over the text you want to format.

- If you're using a touchscreen device, tap and drag over the text you want to format.

- If you're using a keyboard, place the cursor at the beginning of the text you want to format, hold down the Shift key, and then use the right or down arrow keys to select the text. Release the Shift key when you've selected all the text you want.

2. Once you've selected the text, go to the "Format" tab and you'll find these options:

   - **Bold:** Use this to make text stand out with thicker letters.

   - **Italic:** This slants the text slightly to add emphasis.

   - **Underline:** This adds a line under the selected text, but it's best to avoid it for regular text since links are usually underlined by default.

   - **Bulleted list:** Click this button to create a list with bullet points at the beginning of each item.

   - **Numbered list:** Click this button to create a list with numbers at the beginning of each item.

- **Styles:** Choose a style from the drop-down menu to apply multiple formats at once, like making the text bigger and turning it blue.

3. After you've finished formatting the text, you can click the "Send" button to send your email.

Send Files and Pictures

1. Go to the "Insert" tab. This tab has tools for sending files and pictures.

2. To send a file, click on the "Files" button. The "Open" dialog box will appear. Find and select the file you want to send, and then click "Open" in the dialog box. You can send more than one file with the email. In the Compose window, you'll see the files you want to send as thumbnails under the heading "Attachments". If you

change your mind about sending a file, click the X button on that file.

3. To send a picture, first, place the cursor where you want the picture to go in the email. Then click on the "Pictures" button on the Insert tab. The "Open" dialog box will appear. Select the picture you want to send, and then click or tap the "Insert" button.

4. Once you've attached all the files and pictures you want, click the "Send" button to send them with your email.

Read and Respond to Incoming Email

1. To check your email, go to the Start screen and select the Mail tile. This will open the Mail app, and you'll see your inbox, which contains all your received messages.

2. Click on a message in your inbox to read it. The message will open in a new view, and you can read its contents.

3. If you want to reply to the message, click the "Reply" or "Reply All" button. If you want to forward the message to someone else, click the "Forward" button. This will

create a new message with the original message already included. The subject line will automatically start with "RE:" for replies or "FW:" for forwarded messages. You can then type your response and click "Send" to send the message.

4. To manage your messages, you have some options. You can delete a message you no longer need. You can also flag a message to remind yourself to deal with it later. To do this, select the "More" button (three dots) in the upper-right corner of the screen and choose the appropriate option.

5. You can also mark a message as unread if you want it to appear as if you haven't read it yet. This can be helpful if you want to come back to it later. Again, select the "More" button to find this option.

6. If you need to move an email from one folder to another, you can use the "Move" option. Click the "More" button and then select "Move" from the drop-down menu. You can then choose a folder to move the email to from the "Move To" panel.

7. These options give you more control over your emails and help you manage them effectively.

Change Mail Settings

1. To access the Mail settings, first, open the Mail app. Then, click on the Folder panel button in the lower-right corner. After that, click on the Settings button, and the Settings panel will appear on the right side of the screen.

Settings

Manage accounts

Personalization

Automatic replies

Focused inbox

Message list

Reading pane

Signature

Default Font

Notifications

Email security

What's new

Outlook for Android and iOS

Help

Trust Center

Feedback

About

2. In the Settings panel, go to the Accounts section and select "Manage Accounts." Choose the email account for which you want to make changes, and the Account Settings dialog box will appear.

3. In the Account Settings dialog box, you can make the desired changes. You can change the Account Name, which is the name of your email service provider. For example, you can use your name followed by "email" to make it more personal.

4. If you want to change how often the Mail app checks for new emails, click on "Change Mailbox Sync Settings." This will open the Sync Settings dialog box, where you can choose the frequency of email synchronization.

5. If you no longer want to use an email account in the Mail app, you can delete it by selecting "Delete Account." This will remove the account from the app, and you won't receive emails from it anymore.

6. In the Sync Settings dialog box, you can choose how often the Mail app downloads new content, like emails and images. You can set it to every 15 or 30 minutes, hourly, or only when you manually sync.

7. If pictures are not showing in your emails, you can select the option "Always Download Full Message and Internet Images" to fix the issue.

8. You can also set how far back the Mail app downloads messages to your computer by adjusting the "Download Email From" setting. However, this may not be relevant for new email accounts.

9. There are sync options for email, calendar, and contacts. You can turn off email sync if you don't want to receive emails from that account in the Mail app. Similarly, you can turn off calendar and contacts sync for privacy reasons if you don't want the Mail app to access that information from the Calendar app or People app.

CHAPTER 8: SHOPPING AND ORDERING ONLINE

Purchasing from Online Retailers

If you've never shopped online before, you might be curious about how it works. It's actually quite simple! All you need is a computer, a credit card, and a good internet connection.

When you shop online, the process is usually the same, no matter which store you visit. You'll go through a few steps, like browsing for items, adding them to your cart, and then paying for your order at the checkout. It's a straightforward and convenient way to shop from the comfort of your own home.

Discover Online Retailers

To start shopping online, you need to choose where you want to shop. Many big stores like Best Buy, Costco, The Home Depot, Kohl's, Macy's, Office Depot, Nordstrom, Sephora, Target, and Walmart have websites for online shopping. You can also find catalog merchants like Coldwater Creek, L.L. Bean, and Land's End with online ordering options.

Apart from these stores, there are online-only retailers that sell various items. These companies don't have physical stores; they operate solely online and deliver products directly to buyers. Some examples include Amazon.com, Overstock.com, and Wayfair.

Search or Browse for Merchandise

Once you decide where to shop online, you'll need to find the products you want. There are two ways to do this: browsing through categories or using the search feature.

Browsing is like exploring different sections in a regular store. You click on a main category, like "Clothing," and then you can further click on subcategories like "Men's," "Women's," or "Children's" clothing. Keep clicking until you find the specific item you're looking for.

If you already know exactly what you want, using the search box is faster. For example, if you're looking for a women's sweater, just type "women's sweater" in the search box, and you'll see a list of matching items. You can even use filters like color, size, or brand to refine your search.

If you're not sure what you want, browsing might be better. But if you know what you need and want to find it quickly without distractions, using the search feature is the faster option.

Examine the Product (Virtually)

Whether you browse or search for products online, you'll see a list of different items on a web page. But these listings often have short descriptions that may not give you enough information to make a decision.

To learn more about a specific item, click on its link. This will take you to a dedicated product page with a picture and a detailed description of the item. You can also find different views, colors, sizes, additional information, customer reviews, and even optional accessories related to the item.

Reading customer reviews can be helpful too. You can see what other customers liked or didn't like about the product, especially for clothing items to know if they fit well.

If you like what you see on the product page, you can proceed to order it. If not, you can go back to the main product listing by clicking your browser's Back button to explore other options.

Make a Purchase

On each product page, you'll find a button with labels like "Purchase," "Buy Now," "Add to Cart," or something similar. To buy the product, you need to click this "buy" button. Just looking at the product description won't make the purchase; you have to manually click the button to place the order.

When you click the "buy" button, the item is added to your virtual shopping cart, which works like a real-world shopping cart. All the items you choose to buy are put into this virtual cart.

After you add an item to your shopping cart, you can continue shopping for more items on the same website or proceed to the checkout. Keep in mind that adding items to your cart doesn't complete the purchase yet. You can keep shopping and adding more items to your cart as long as you want.

If you change your mind or don't want to buy anything right away, you can leave the website without making a purchase. It's like leaving your shopping cart in a physical store and walking out without buying anything. You won't be charged for anything until you go through the checkout process. Some websites may keep the items in your cart for the next time you visit, so you don't have to start over when you come back.

Check Out and Pay

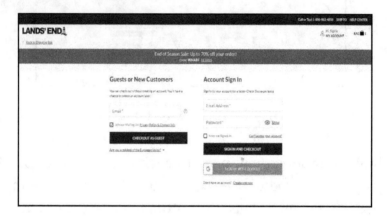

To complete your purchase, you need to go to the store's checkout. It's like going to the checkout line in a regular store, where you pay for your items.

The checkout process on an online store involves filling out some forms. If you've shopped there before, it might remember some of your information. Otherwise, you'll need to enter your name, address, phone number, and the shipping address if it's different from your billing address. You'll also need to provide your credit card number to pay for the items.

During checkout, you can review your order and make changes if needed. You can remove items you don't want or change the quantities. Some stores even offer gift-wrapping options if you're sending the items as presents.

You may have different shipping options, like regular or expedited shipping, sometimes with free shipping for orders above a certain amount. Some stores may group items for reduced shipping costs, but be careful if an item is out of stock, as it could delay the whole order.

Once you've entered all the information, you'll click a button to place your order. You might see a confirmation screen with your order number. Keep this number in case you need to contact customer service. The store will also send you a confirmation email with the same information.

That's it! You shop, check out, and pay, and your order should arrive within the expected time. It's a straightforward process!

Buying and Selling at Online Marketplaces

Besides traditional retailers, there are online marketplaces where individuals can buy and sell goods to each other. It's like an online garage sale, where you can find unique items from other people and also sell things you no longer need.

Craigslist

Craigslist is like an online version of classified ads in a newspaper. People list items they want to sell, and you can contact them through Craigslist to arrange the purchase.

On Craigslist, you need to deal directly with the seller for payment, usually with cash. It's best for buying and selling locally, where you can meet up with the seller to get the items in person. It's not for buying or selling items that need to be shipped.

You can also use Craigslist to sell things you have. In many categories, it's free to list your items for sale.

eBay

eBay is an online marketplace where you can buy and sell items. It used to be mostly an auction site, where you bid for items and the highest bidder wins. But now, you can also find items for sale at a fixed price, just like buying from a regular online store.

When you buy from an eBay seller, you make your payment through eBay, and they have a buyer protection plan to help if there are any issues. However, buying from individual sellers might not always be as safe or smooth as buying from a regular store. Some sellers don't accept returns, for example.

Unlike Craigslist, which is mainly for local sales, eBay sellers can ship items across the country and even worldwide. You can find items from individual sellers and also from big retailers on eBay.

You can also sell your own items on eBay. You pay a fee to list the item, and if it sells, you pay another fee.

Etsy

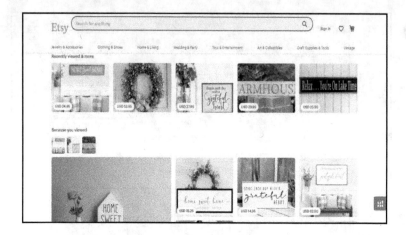

Etsy is an online store where people sell handmade and vintage items like artwork, clothes, jewelry, and more. The sellers are usually individuals who create these items themselves and sell them on Etsy. When you buy something on Etsy, you can pay with a credit card, debit card, or PayPal through the website.

If you make your own items, Etsy is a good place to sell them. It's similar to eBay where you pay a fee to list your item for sale, and when it sells, you also pay a transaction fee.

Facebook Marketplace

If you're on Facebook, you can use the Facebook Marketplace (www.facebook.com/marketplace) to buy and sell things. It's similar to Craigslist, where you can list items you want to sell, but you don't actually buy or sell through Facebook.

If you want to buy something from the Facebook Marketplace, you need to contact the seller directly (who is also a Facebook member) to arrange payment and pick up. Most transactions are done with cash. Just like with Craigslist, you need to be careful when buying something from the Facebook Marketplace.

To sell on the Facebook Marketplace, you create a listing for the item you want to sell, and the best part is that there are no fees involved.

Reverb

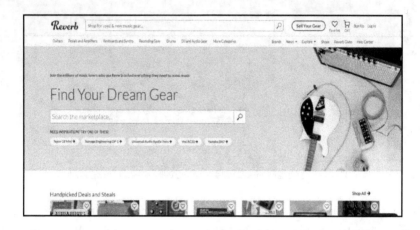

Reverb (www.reverb.com) is an online marketplace for musical instruments, DJ gear, and recording equipment. It's popular among musicians and those involved in the music industry.

On Reverb, you can buy items from both individual sellers and music stores. When you make a purchase, you pay through Reverb using a credit/debit card or PayPal. The site has a buyer protection plan, but be cautious when buying from individuals as there could be issues with the item.

If you want to sell used musical instruments and gear, Reverb is a great place because you have a targeted audience. There are no fees for listing items, but when you make a sale, Reverb charges a 5% fee and a 2.5% to 2.7% payment processing fee.

Ordering Meals, Groceries, and More for Delivery

During the COVID-19 crisis, when many of us had to stay at home, we relied on our computers to order food, groceries, and other items for delivery. It became really convenient to shop online and have everything delivered right to our doorstep. You don't need to go out anymore!

A lot of grocery stores, pharmacies, and restaurants have their own delivery services or work with local or national delivery companies. To order, you usually visit their website, pick what you want, and select the delivery option.

Order Meals Online

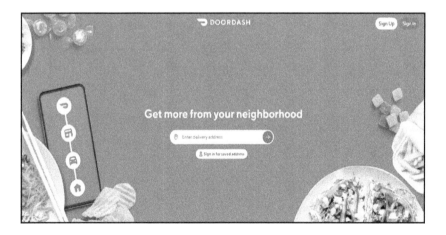

Nowadays, a lot of restaurants offer delivery services. But remember, these deliveries usually come with a cost. You'll need to pay a delivery fee and, if you want, add a tip for the driver. You'll pay for everything online when you place your order. You can use your credit or debit card or even PayPal to make the payment.

Some restaurants have their own delivery drivers, while others use services like DoorDash, Grubhub, or UberEats to handle the deliveries.

You can order directly from the restaurant or sometimes use the delivery service's website or app. After you order and pay online, they'll give you an estimated time for your delivery. You might also get an email or link to a page where you can track the status of your order and even see where the delivery driver is on a map.

When you order, some restaurants give you the option of normal or contactless delivery. Normal delivery means the driver will bring the food to your door and hand it to you. With contactless delivery, they'll leave the food at your doorstep and let you know when it's there, so there's no direct contact with the driver. You get to choose which option you prefer when you place your order.

Order Groceries Online

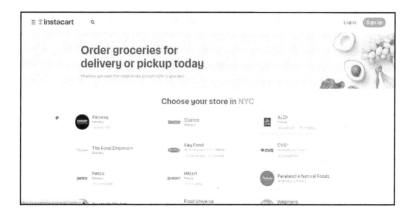

A lot of grocery stores now offer a service where you can order your groceries online and have them delivered to your home. It's similar to ordering food delivery from a restaurant, but there are more choices available.

You can go to the grocery store's website and place your order there. They usually have everything available online that they have in their physical stores, like fresh meats, vegetables, bakery items, and other groceries. If your first choice isn't available, they might ask you to pick an alternative brand or size.

Some bigger grocery chains have their own delivery drivers, but others use services like InstaCart or Shipt to handle the deliveries. There might be a delivery fee, and you can also choose to tip the delivery driver. Since some groceries need to be kept cold, the store will let you pick a delivery time that works for you, so you can be home to receive the groceries.

CONCLUSION

Windows 11 provides seniors with an accessible computing experience that leverages the familiar Windows interface. Thanks to its clean design, intuitive navigation tools, enhanced accessibility features and tightened security settings, Windows 11 enables older PC users to make the most of their PCs. This guide has given seniors the core skills required to use Windows 11. We began by exploring basic functions such as opening apps, adjusting volume levels, and shutting off computers. Seniors learned how to navigate the newly redesigned Start menu, search for apps, and customize their Start screen layout. Security and privacy were emphasized with lessons about managing user accounts such as signing in with Microsoft and local accounts, creating household member accounts, creating household passwords, and setting strong passwords.

At an orientation of the desktop interface, seniors were introduced to how they could change settings, arrange windows efficiently with Snap Layouts, and pin their favorite applications to the taskbar. Web browsing enables seniors to gain access to information online; so we presented using Microsoft Edge for search, open tabs, bookmark sites, block ads, etc. E-mail keeps us connected; so instructions were also given on creating messages using Mail app with attachments of files or photos and customizing settings accordingly for optimal use.

The guide concluded with guidance on shopping and ordering safely online, from making purchases at major retailers to ordering groceries for delivery. With this foundation in place, seniors can use Windows 11 computers to keep in contact with loved ones, pursue hobbies and interests online, maintain independence, and remain independent. Starting with fundamentals discussed here will build confidence through practice and discovery; when needed refer back for review when needed - learning Windows 11 opens a whole world of potential possibilities through technology!